THIS BOOK IS FOR

. . . .

THE MOST MISERABLE/INTENSE/
ATTRACTIVE/BORING/EROTIC/
DELIGHTFUL LIBRA LOVER I KNOW.
FROM

. . . .

P.S. TAKE A GOOD LOOK AT PAGE(S)

. . . .

LIBRA

A CORGI BOOK 0 552 12844 9

First publication in Great Britain
PRINTING HISTORY
Corgi edition published 1986

Corgi Books are published by Transworld Publishers Ltd.,
61-63 Uxbridge Road, Ealing, London W5 5SA, in Australia by
Transworld Publishers (Australia) Pty. Ltd., 15-23 Helles Avenue,
Moorebank, NSW 2170, and in New Zealand by Transworld
Publishers (N.Z.) Ltd., Cnr. Moselle and Waipareira Avenues,
Henderson, Auckland.

Made and printed in Great Britain by the
Guernsey Press Co. Ltd., Guernsey, Channel Islands.

Ian Heath's
LOVE SIGNS
LIBRA

CORGI BOOKS

LIBRA

SEPTEMBER 23 - OCTOBER 22

SEVENTH SIGN OF THE ZODIAC
SYMBOL : THE SCALES
RULING PLANET : VENUS
NUMBER : SIX
COLOURS : PASTEL PINK , BLUE
FLOWER : LILY
DAY : FRIDAY
GEMS : TURQUOISE , BLUE OPAL
METAL : COPPER

The LIBRAN lover is . . . .

. . . . STUBBORN . . . .

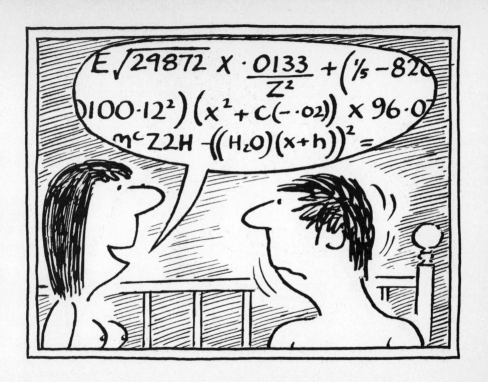

. . . . CLEVER . . . .

...A GOOD CONVERSATIONALIST...

...........FAIR............

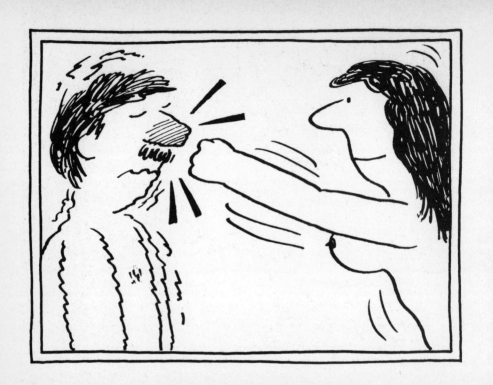

. . . . DIPLOMATIC . . . .

. . . . PEACE-LOVING . . . .

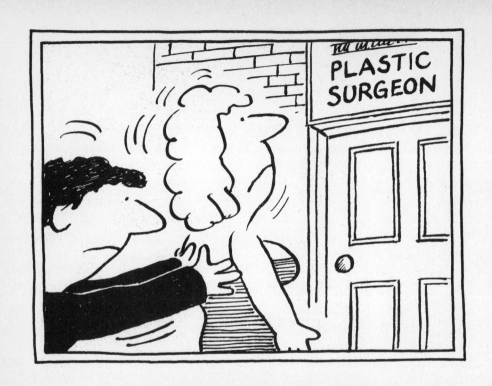

. . . . A PERFECTIONIST . . . .

. . . . AND HELPFUL.

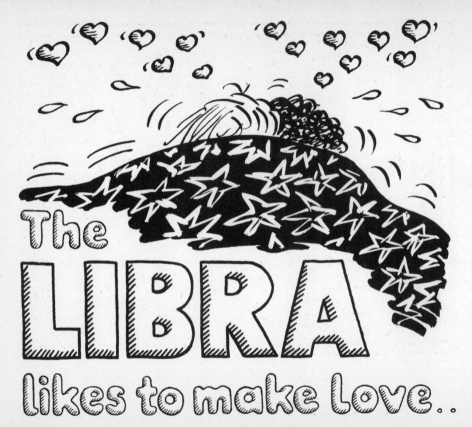

The **LIBRA** likes to make love..

14

. . . . .ON WATER-SKIS. . . . .

. . . . IN A THUNDERSTORM . . . . . .

. . . . . .ON A PARK BENCH. . . . . . .

. . . . .UNDER CANVAS. . . . .

. . . . . . IN A SUPERMARKET. . . . . .

. . . . . AND IN A GYMNASIUM.

. . . . .IS CANDLELIT. . . . .

. . . . . . .HAS PIPED MUSIC. . . . .

..... AND A COCKTAIL BAR.

MMMMMMMM

To turn on
a male
LIBRA.....

25

. . . . WEAR GLASSES. . . . .

. . . . . . HIGH-HEELED SHOES . . . . .

. . . . AND TIGHT SKIRTS.

MMMMMMMM

To turn on
a female
LIBRA......

. . . . KEEP FIT. . . . .

. . . . .GROW A BEARD. . . . .

. . .AND WEAR NO AFTER-SHAVE.

EEEEEEEEEEEEE! OOOOOOOOOO!

LIBRAN

erogenous zones are.....

. . . . . . .THE BUTTOCKS. . . . .

. . . . ARMPITS . . . .

. . . . . . .SMALL OF THE BACK. . . . . . .

. . . . AND LEFT KNEE.

APHRODISIACS
FOR THE ♡
LIBRAN LOVER

BRANDY SNAPS

CHOCOLATE LOG
AND CUSTARD

AFTER-DINNER MINTS

PRAWN CRACKERS

JELLY

The LIBRAN lover likes to receive....

. . . . . . CHILLED CHAMPAGNE . . . . . .

. . . . .A VENUS FLYTRAP. . . . .

. . . . AND A TIE-PIN.

LIBRA AND LOVERS

HEART RATINGS

♡♡♡♡♡ POW!! ZAP!!

♡♡♡♡ MAGIC~BUT NOT 'IT'

♡♡♡ FUN! FUN! FUN!

♡♡ PRETTY AWFUL

♡ GRIM~RUN FAST!

LIBRA and...

...ARIES

BOTH LOVE THE PHYSICAL PART,
BUT BOREDOM SOON SETS IN.
AN IDEAL SHORT-TERM UNION.

...TAURUS

AN IMPOSSIBLE MATCH,
OVER BEFORE IT'S BEGUN.

LIBRA and...

...GEMINI

AN EXPERIENCE, DESTINED TO LAST.

♡ ♡ ♡ ♡ ♡

...CANCER

NOT A LOT GOING FOR THESE TWO!

♡ ♡

...LEO

AN ENTERTAINING TIME FOR THIS
PAIR! AND POSSIBLY LONG-TERM.

♡ ♡ ♡ ♡

LIBRA and ...

... VIRGO

INTERESTING FOR QUITE A WHILE.
WITH LOTS OF EFFORT ON BOTH SIDES
THIS COULD BE 'IT.'

♡ ♡ ♡ ♡

... LIBRA

A FUN AFFAIR,
BUT PROBABLY ONLY A SHORT ONE.

♡ ♡ ♡

o o o o o o o o o o o o o o o o o o o o o o

LIBRA and . . .

. . . SCORPIO

A SIZZLING COMBINATION,
WITH PLENTY OF PROMISE FOR
THOSE WHO LIKE IT HOT!

♡ ♡ ♡ ♡

. . . SAGITTARIUS

AN EXCITING LIASON
WITH MUCH FUN AND GAMES.

♡ ♡ ♡ ♡

o o o o o o o o o o o o o o o o o o

LIBRA and...

...CAPRICORN

AN ENJOYABLE AFFAIR — FOR A TIME.

♡ ♡ ♡

...AQUARIUS

SIZZLING! DYNAMIC! BEAUTIFUL!

♡ ♡ ♡ ♡ ♡

...PISCES

NO! NO! NO!

♡

o o o o o o o o o o o o o o o o o o o o o o

Annoying **LIBRAN** habits are......

. . . . . TALKING IN THEIR SLEEP. . . . .

...SINGING ALONG TO RECORDS...

. . . . . . .AND TWITCHING.

FAMOUS LIBRAN LOVERS

JERRY LEE LEWIS · OSCAR WILDE

MAHATMA GANDHI · T.S. ELLIOT

JOHN LENNON · RULA LENSKA

FRANZ LISZT · CHARLTON HESTON

ARTHUR MILLER · PETER FINCH

OLIVIA NEWTON-JOHN
WALTER MATTHAU · GORE VIDAL
BRIGITTE BARDOT · HAROLD PINTER
MICKEY ROONEY · RICHARD HARRIS
LILY LANGTRY · CHUBBY CHECKER
BUSTER KEATON · PIERRE TRUDEAU
CHARLIE BROWN · GROUCHO MARX
DEBORAH KERR · CLIFF RICHARD
GEORGE GERSHWIN · BILL TIDY
F. SCOTT FITZGERALD

To keep your
LIBRAN
lover......

56

. . . . . . SPARE NO EXPENSE. . . . . . .

. . . . BE ATTENTIVE . . . .

. . . . .CUDDLE A LOT.

To get rid of your **LIBRAN** lover........

. . . . PUT ON WEIGHT.

. . . . .NAG. . . . .

. . . . FLIRT.